COMMUNITY-LED TEAM

How to Create a Team that Leads Itself

Karl-Johan Spiik has during his career worked for over a decade in community-led teams, usually in the role of a coaching leader. He has participated more than 60 projects in teams of different sizes. Karl-Johan trains teams and organizations to work in a more agile way in a continuously changing environment. Karl-Johan's basic values and knowledge focus on ways of avoiding hurry and stress by improving the working methods. Tools for all this are project leadership, his own experience, and community-led orientation.

Author website:
www.johtajuushakkeri.fi/en

KARL-JOHAN SPIIK

COMMUNITY-LED TEAM

How to Create
a Team that Leads Itself

KARLEX

2023

Publisher: Karlex Oy
Design and Illustrations: Eve Sillanpää
Photographer: Jouni Kuru
Translation by: Kaarina Valtanen and Henrik Andergård

ISBN 978-952-69963-7-0 (softcover)
ISBN 978-952-69963-8-7 (PDF)
ISBN 978-952-69963-9-4 (MP3)

CONTENT

FOREWORD

During my own career I have worked for over a decade in community-led teams, usually in the role of coaching leader. I have taken part in about fifty projects with teams of different sizes. I have been involved in projects with teams and people from several organizations. In all cases and teams the same principles arise, communication being the cornerstone.

Some years ago, I started to work in an expert organization with no supervisor. I noticed that the model of working in a team functioned well not only in small teams but also in cases where there were hundreds of people cooperating. I wanted to develop my understanding of teamwork. Soon after starting the work, I began to make weekly notes based on my own experiences about team leadership. After some months a certain model formed that I returned to in all my notes.

First, I named that model the hierarchy of self-management. I have always loved Maslow's Hierarchy of Needs despite the criticism targeted at it. Both models have similar structures. The lower levels need to be fulfilled in order to develop the higher levels. If something isn't working on the lower level, that thing must be corrected first.

Later, when I was finishing my online course, a consultant helping me said that my model had too many levels. It looked confusing and the reader could not understand it. So, I then divided the eight basic levels into three stairs and each stair into steps. The model developed further, and it became more understandable, which helped to improve the planning of the online course.

The hierarchy of self-management – the eight basic levels of a community-led team The team starts from the lowest level and progresses upwards level by level.

The online course based on my team model was ready in the beginning of 2021. I wanted to be the first to provide a practical tool for the activity of a community-lead team.

The Model of Activities for a Community-Led Team

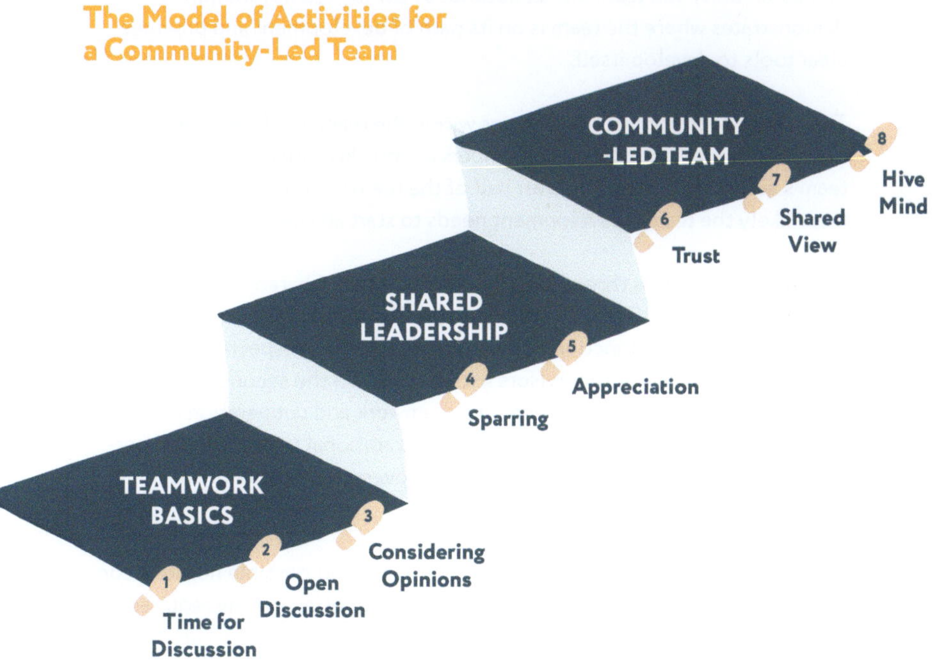

The model for a community-led team: three stairs and eight steps. The team will start from the bottom and go forward upwards. If the requirements of one step are not met, then the team has to return to a lower step.

A model is a model, and it is not supposed to be read literally. This team model gives a good grasp on how one's own team is placed in relation to its own development. At its best, it is a fine tool that the team can use to develop itself and to improve cooperation. The most important thing is to remember that the activities of the whole team are based on well-being and trust.

INTRODUCTION

The community-led team model describes how the teams function. It demonstrates where the team is on its path of development and provides clear tools to develop itself.

The model does not include changes within the team itself, because in a community-led team the new members are quickly integrated into the team's activities. However, if over half of the team members are replaced, most likely the team's development needs to start all over again.

The model comprises three stairs: Teamwork Basics, Shared Leadership, and Community-Led Team. On the first stair Teamwork Basics, all the basic matters needed for a functioning team are inspected, irrespective of the presence or absence of supervisors in that team. On the second stair Shared Leadership, various matters concerning teamwork and cooperation are trained. This middle stair is also suitable for traditional teams with a supervisor. The third stair Community-Led Team covers the aspects of coaching leadership and not having a supervisor.

On the two lower stairs, the team's requirements, and possible negative consequences if those are not met, are inspected. Sometimes some requirement is not met at all, but the team can still proceed to the next step. Each team can agree on which consequences are acceptable within the team. In work life projects, there are often recognized risks. The threats presented in this book are to be considered in the same way. It is advised to make a plan of recovery, which will be initiated in case a risk becomes reality.

On the top stair of this model, there are no requirements presented for the team anymore, but some characteristics of a community-led team. That team is based on the internal motivation of its members and their willingness to work together without any supervisor. When the team reaches the top level, the meaning of the requirements and the model itself fades away, as the team gets inspired into the state of flow and notices that it has now reached the top step.

Each step has concrete actions as examples for how to make the team meet all the requirements or characteristics needed.

After the presentation of the stairs, this book will cover how the model is applicable to different teams, what roles there are in the team, and how the model can be used to support the teamwork. The model is mainly meant to be introduced to the teams during the monthly reflective workshops.

TEAMWORK BASICS

The first stair includes matters that should be in order in all teams. If the requirements of this stair are not met, then the team is not a team but just a unit of the organization or a group of people whose actions are just bundled together.

Each team needs to understand the meaning of presence, communication, and cooperation. It is important to keep these basic themes up, and to speak up if there are any issues about them. Going through these themes before founding the team is vital to make the practices meet the expectations.

If there are a lot of struggles with the problems on this stair, it is good to admit that the team is only in its early phase of development. When putting the basics in order each team member is directed to look in the mirror and grow as a person. The meaning of presence is emphasized, and the team starts to build up its future together. If there are continuous problems on this stair, it is time to check whether the team in its present form is worth keeping or not. A team without a supervisor cannot have a soloist team member who does not cooperate with the other members.

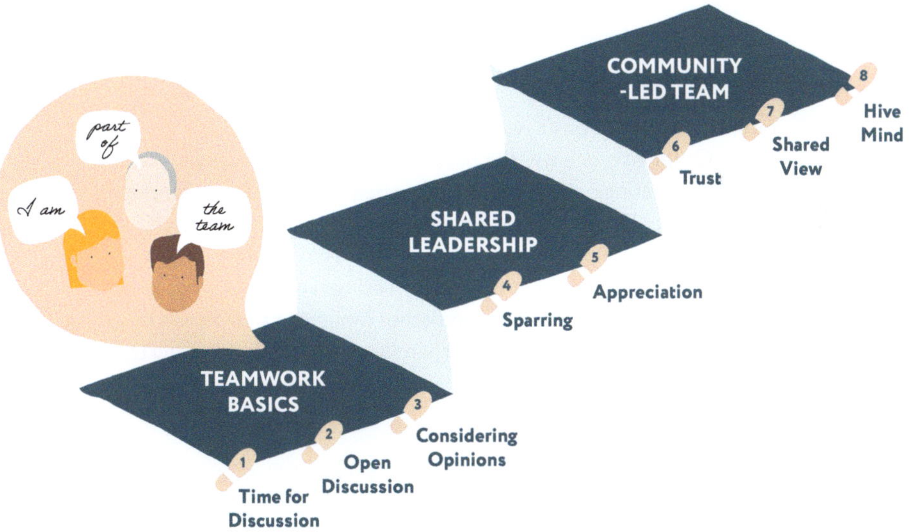

The lowest stair Teamwork basics. This stair comprises three parts or steps
- giving time to discussion, open discussion and considering opinions.

Time for Discussion

The goal is to get all the team members available at the team's joint meetings. The team is a team when it does things together and communicates about them. Not all tasks concern all team members, but the team meetings are a uniting factor for the team. The members need to understand their own role and meaning in the team and show it to the others by being present and available at the team meetings.

- 👉 *Prioritize the team meetings*
- 👉 *Notify the team about your absences*
- 👉 *Honor the agreed timetables*
- 👉 *End meetings at the agreed times*

REQUIREMENTS

+ Managing one's own work

Everyone is to manage one's work and workload. Otherwise, one will not have time nor interest to participate in joint team meetings. Life is a challenge when one has a lot to handle at the same time. This is when one needs the skills to manage oneself and to use one's calendar. A team member needs to be able to schedule their workload to be present at the team meetings and actually focus on them. Sometimes one can be busy and other thoughts can fill one's head but if this is a constant state of mind, then there is something wrong the managing one's own work.

+ The meetings are not to exceed the agreed time

The agreed matters are respected and followed without any exceptions. This is a prerequisite and a starting point. When a meeting time is agreed, the team sticks to it and the time reserved for it is respected and ended on time. If the meeting time is not enough to cover everything at hand, the members are asked whether the meeting can continue, or a new meeting time is agreed for later. If repeatedly the time seems to run out, then there is something wrong in the preparation of the meeting (too short a time or matters poorly prepared).

When the matters at hand are dealt with and done, the meeting ends and the members can get back to their own tasks. There is no point holding the whole team to listen to a dialogue between
just some people.

+ Everyone prioritizes the team meetings

All members will be present when the meetings start. Each has the meetings marked in their calendars, and they are prioritized and never overridden by other tasks. If one really must have another meeting at the same time, one then must ask the team members whether it would be possible to reschedule the team meeting. Nowadays, with the shared calendars any team member could transfer the team meeting to a timeslot available for everyone in the team.

+ Time reserved for shared matters

When some shared matter needs handling by several team members, a meeting needs to be set up. Small matters can be handled in other ways like via chat or e-mail, but as a basic principle, any more complicated matters call for a meeting or a shared online phone call. Then it is important to gather the members together to discuss the matter and make a clear, common decision, rather than to postpone the matter for hours or even days in message chains. It is possible to cover various smaller matters at the team meetings, but when there are larger issues it is advisable to reserve dedicated time for them. Larger matters and entities demanding their own meetings are, e.g., resourcing, planning sales, or reflecting on actions.

TEAMWORK
BASICS

- One member takes care of everything for the team

When matters are not handled together or
they are inefficiently circulated for too long, then all members no
longer take part in decision-making. I do not mean a situation where
a member wants to recuse themselves from it, but when the communication within the team is on a poor level. One person takes over the
responsibility for the team and starts to take care of matters. Gradually,
the others get used to this, do not participate anymore and then the
team slides back to a traditional model with a supervisor.

There is nothing wrong with the model of having a supervisor when it
was the choice to start with. But in that case, one must understand that
the team members do not commit themselves to decisions nor do they
feel any ownership for them.

Team leaders often worry about the non-commitment of the team
members. This lack of commitment is the result of the fact that the
team members do not listen to the opinions of other team members,
and do not act for the team but for oneself. When each member gets
to decide and is involved in the process, there is high motivation and
mutual respect for the colleague, as they are doing something for the
other team members.

- The team is just a unit in the organization

If the team members never gather for meetings, they will never form
a tight team. There are some organizations where the teams only play
an apparent role in dividing the larger departments into smaller units.
The team members report to each other or the team, but do not really
cooperate as such. The first thing in the development of the team is to
gather the members and to have them communicate with each other. If
the team members are not repeatedly available at the team meetings,
the group cannot work as a team.

- Motivation to prioritize the team meetings vanishes

When one or more members of the team make their own choices and repeatedly don't show up at the team meetings, this influences the others' motivation. In the team it should not be allowed to let someone act solo as they please. No excuse can be so important that it would prevent one taking part in the team meetings. If the team cannot control its member, it must give them a "time-out" or even remove them from the team entirely.

Nobody is to have a preferential role in the team. Sometimes a member knows something better than the others, helps them out and may get some special rights due to the special skills. The team may always negotiate the rules together, but being present at the meetings is not negotiable. The team is not a team if not all the members are present at the meetings.

Open Discussion

When there is trust in the team that all members will by default be present at the meetings, it is possible to build up the basis of communication. Everyone should open their mouths and talk about their tasks in the team. Sometimes it is possible to exchange ideas their but speaking should be the number one way to communicate about one's work and opinions. If the team is working online, it is vital that sound and video are used.

A person's communication is based on all five senses, and usually only two are in use in an online meeting. Encountering someone is really challenging if their message is just some text somewhere. The team cannot know about their state of mind nor experience that they are being open to others if they are hiding behind a curtain and repeatedly giving excuses for refusing to turn the camera on. When someone is avoiding contact, it creates concern and doubt in the others and then there is no trust within the team.

The team cannot work as a team if the members are hiding from each other and communicating only minimally. The team members must be able to face each other.

To start the meeting, take a round to ask "How are you doing?"

If there is a hard subject on the agenda, warm up the members first with a light exercise

Encourage everyone to express their opinion, do not let anyone withdraw from the discussion

REQUIREMENTS

+ Everyone must have a chance to express one's opinion

All the circumstances and tools of the members must be on such a level that everyone has a chance to express their opinion. Others need to give space and let each team member speak their mind. If one member seems to dominate, the other members need to help the more silent ones to express themselves.

Each member of the team has a duty to encourage the others to state their opinion and prevent any withdrawal. One good way to activate the members is to take a round asking "How are you doing?" This way everyone gets to say something about a familiar and safe matter.

+Everyone needs to dare say one's opinion

Every team member needs to be physically (or remotely online) and mentally present. Everyone needs to secure the working environment so that they have the best possible prerequisites and chances to express their true feelings. So, it is an individual's own responsibility to control their own feelings and state of mind, and at least to communicate about them in case they are having a bad day, and some pointed opinions may emerge.

If there is a difficult theme to be discussed at the meeting, it is advised to first do a warm-up task. This helps to create a sense of community and a safe atmosphere for all, so that moving onto the actual matter gets easier.

+ Do not criticize others' opinions

"Everyone is equal, but everyone's ideas are not equal" is a good sentence but not applicable on this stair. There is a big difference whether one criticizes others' opinions or ponders upon the values of two different ideas for the working life.

When others are talking about their opinions, all the members in the team need to accept that these opinions do not always match. Criticizing others' opinions also includes expressions of body language, like rolling one's eyes. Each member needs to control oneself even if the other's opinion causes irritation.

+ All matters are subject to be discussed

Sometimes there is not enough time to discuss all matters. Other times some matters are better to deal with later when the dust has

settled. However, the team must not have any matters that cannot be discussed at all. It is not possible to have a matter or topic suppressed time after time.

+ Everyone should be themselves

The team members cannot hide themselves behind a role. The above-mentioned requirements are not met if the team member is not themselves. Each of us has a work role, home role and other roles. That is ok, but it is not good to hide weaknesses behind a role in working life. The team member needs to understand and recognize if they are about to get into a disruptive role. And then, the other members can mention this in private so that the person gets a chance to review themselves and their actions.

THREATS

- Not expressing one's own opinion

If there is no room for discussion or safety
to express one's own opinion in the team, it may leave some opinions unspoken. The underlying reason may be fear of criticism or mockery. Even the smallest signs of body language may cause an unpleasant feeling for sensitive members, even for weeks, and cause them to shut down so that they do not express their opinion.

- Bringing out one's own opinion in a provocative manner

A team member may express their opinion in such a way that the others get irritated. The cause behind this may be that they don't feel good about themselves and choose to attack in order to protect them-selves, or they may have needed to express their opinions sharply in other areas of life to get ideas through to someone. Usually, a member with a role like this makes the others defensive, so they are not creating a safe nor trusting atmosphere. The basis for a cooperative team is open communication, which is inhibited by a provocative role.

- Irritation arises from differing opinions

When one's own state of mind is a bit off, or one is feeling awful or unsafe, the opinions of others may cause irritation. And when that happens, we start to react – subconsciously or consciously. The reaction is visible in body language and at its worst in dismissive comments and criticism.

Others' opinions may also irritate us when we are afraid of being left alone, when the opinions of others differ from ours, or an unpleasant process is initiated within us only for us to notice we were wrong after all.

- No discussion about the actual matter

If the theme is a delicate matter, or there are some tensions in the team and the warm-up task was forgotten, the team may end up in an argument. This may easily cause some unfruitful quarreling. Authority may be used, and hard words may be used seemingly about work matters, when the underlying cause is something totally different. This is why a warm-up task and creating a safe environment are so vital.

On the other hand, if the team is in a hurry, it is better to leave some items for later than cover everything and create a bad feeling for everyone. Furthermore, every now and then the matter at hand may demand so much creativity, and a new way of thinking, that the best solution is to leave it to simmer and for the subconscious to process.

- No open discussion arises

The function of the team is based on communication. And communication is based on openness and open discussion, without which the existence of the team is jeopardized.

There are always people in a team who do not understand the importance of the team requirements and think that a bit of goading is allowed. As there is no supervisor in the team, everyone and especially the strongest members should act as a buffer in these cases. It is good to go through these matters with all members, either in one-to-one sessions or if needed, with the whole team present.

Considering Opinions

When everybody is present and says what they are thinking, it is time to start listening to their words. Teamwork does not mean that one comes to listen to others just to get to talk about one's own matters in turn.

While listening to others, it is good to write down some notes and, in the future, to change one's own activities based on the team discussions. After getting direct feedback it is, at the latest, time to ponder one's own actions. However, acting in a proactive way based on others' comments results in the best teamwork.

When a team member refers to someone else's comments from a previous meeting and gives credit to how the comments helped and improved their own work, it creates a grateful atmosphere and provides an uplifting example. The feedback does not have to be immediate. When the team learns that the uttered words matter, they start to communicate more. There is no need to question whether the others are listening or not.

REQUIREMENTS

+ All opinions are equal

Everybody understands that all opinions are equal. On this stair all opinions are accepted without grumbling and are pondered upon even if they would conflict with one's own thoughts. One can separate opinions and facts. Sometimes it is understood that a member's opinion may be seen as fact by them, in which case there is no use arguing about it. By showing empathy and commenting even if we think differently, we show that we respect the team member. This could be carried out so that one comments positively on their proposals and by emphasizing those parts that one supports even if the whole idea does not sound good as such.

+ Matters are matters and people are people

There is an understanding in the team that all members are equal, but everyone's ideas are not always equal. When the team is pondering the best way to act or what's best of the team, and one's own idea is not supported, it is not a statement about the person behind the idea. There is a common professional respect between the team members which facilitates discussing matters just as they are. Nobody's ideas should be taken into consideration just so that they don't get upset.

+ Matters intended for discussion are to be prioritized

When there is a lot of work and busy schedules burden the team, it is necessary to prioritize which matters to deal with at the team meetings. If the agenda of the meeting or the team's task list has more items than there is time to deal with, prioritizing is necessary. The team needs to agree on the criteria for how to prioritize. By considering the criteria the most important matters are chosen, and the rest are moved to the next meeting. Even if some matter is a heartfelt topic for a team member, this is not a valid reason to include in the criteria.

+ Feedback from the others affects one's own actions

Each team member is obligated to listen to other members' words and comments. The team cannot work as a team unless the members actively learn from other members' actions. When you get feedback, write down e.g. how you changed your actions. Then at the next meeting you can tell how you have tried to change your actions and what you noticed as a result. The proposals for change do not always improve actions, and that is also a perfectly acceptable outcome. The most important thing here is to show the others that we are doing this together and proposals for change pay attention to what you say.

+ Everyone is ready to justify their own points and opinions

The matters on the meeting's agenda should be well thought-out beforehand – at least the presenter is ready to ponder why to bring up the matter at hand. The team is a safe network to practice justifying

one's point. When matters are being presented and opinions stated, it is likely to end up in conflict-like situations. Sometimes feelings may even heat up. This is quite a normal outcome in all human communication. When the requirements stated earlier are met, each team member can justify their own opinion, and not react negatively if they can't have things their way. The team often concludes later in the process that without jointly considering the matter a completely wrong solution might have been chosen for the problem at hand.

THREATS

- Discussion is futile

The communication in the team remains
superficial with compliments shared and everyone talking about just their own matters. The actual benefit of teamwork, synergy, is not harnessed. The team gathering together should always initiate something more than just working alone would create. A futile discussion does not help anybody but creates a mere illusion of a good team spirit. For some people this is enough, but usually a deeper
cooperation is desired.

- Asking for others' opinion only out of courtesy

Just repeating a learned behavior, attending the meeting, and pretending to listen. Nodding and answering superficially to questions, but thinking only about one's own agenda and trying to get that through by ignoring the others. Having presented that own matter, asking for opinions only because that is the common habit there. Any potential feedback is ignored, not even written down, and the feedback does not change the results.

- Getting into conflicts, which makes cooperation harder

Conflicts are the result of not valuing the opinion of another member. Many are so sure about their own agenda and professional skills that they will not even listen to others nor consider any other angles on the matter. Sometimes it becomes possible to communicate, but because one can't justify one's own point of view, it only leads to quarrel driven by feelings and not solutions. Wanting to be right and to show the other person that you're not giving in.

- The team does not develop, and activity is stagnant

The team only works as a group of people that come together from time to time to tell the others what they have done. They may ask for help when they cannot solve a problem alone or can't cope with the workload. However, asking for help is the last option, and attending the meetings only a habit. When the team does not develop at the team level, members soon start to question the importance of the team meetings. After that the team falls back onto the first step, when some members stop attending the meetings.

- Not being able to prepare for challenging situations

When the team does not communicate, ask questions, or consider the comments made by other members, it cannot prepare for situations arising in the work life. The team should by itself simulate different kinds of situations and practice how to cope with surprising situations. If the team's internal communication doesn't take others into consideration nor learn from their comments, its members are likely to behave accordingly in real situations as well. If they are not prepared to face differing opinions, the team members may also be irritated by questions coming from outsiders as well.

One of the most important things for the team is to take in the culture of gratitude. This means that at the team meetings colleagues are thanked for e.g. help received during the previous week. It doesn't matter whether the well-done task was self-initiated or ordered, as it is always good to receive appreciation. When a few brave members

start this habit and stick to it consistently, it will spread to the whole team. This will be facilitated by agreeing that everyone reserves time for gratitude. Usually, it is necessary to write down the reason for gratitude when it arises instead of leaving it just up to memory. Generally, the team meetings are on Mondays after the weekend, and it may be hard to remember all the help received the previous week right when it is your turn to speak.

When positive matters are focused on, they are reinforced as well. Praising others and showing empathy In small ways. Usually these small ways are gestures, small filler words, or comments that might otherwise be left unsaid. Reinforcing positive experiences works by example, just like swearing. It is contagious. When one lives daily in an environment of praising other members, everyone starts to behave the same way. Good manners are allowed to be spread to the rest of the team, and it could be mutually agreed that there is no need to feel embarrassed about learning how to handle praise. We all had to learn that from somewhere over the years, nobody got that skill as a birth gift.

SHARED LEADERSHIP

Sparring

s. 29

Appreciation

s. 35

When the team's basic matters are in order, it is time to move onto the second stair of the model. By shared leadership the team starts to understand how the team members need each other to reach the goals.

As the basic matters are being put into order, it may still feel like teamwork is a burden and that it does not enhance the actual work. On the second stair, however, the team starts to benefit from the cooperation and begins to understand why and how the results just are better when doing things together. The team members get to know each other and thus create a team spirit. The team gets it routines in shape and forms an identity for itself.

Shared leadership is also suitable for traditional teams with a supervisor. The team may use the model and its tasks presented here, no matter how the team is organized. Shared leadership will help the team understand that the work is done together, and create practices to ask for help if needed. At the same time a mutual respect towards one another awakens within the team. Mistakes are no longer feared like on the lower stairs, but they are brought more and more openly into discussion. The team members consider teamwork rewarding and want to learn more as a unit.

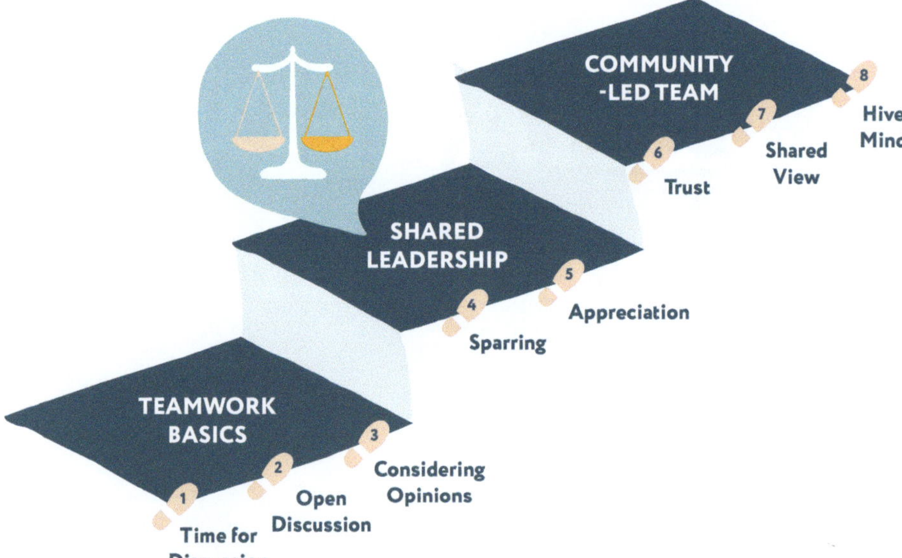

On the middle stair of the team model leadership is shared between the team members. Shared leadership requires sparring and appreciation.

Sparring

The idea of this stair is to get to know the other team members. This stair prepares the members to share leadership together.

The team members know each other well only after they have worked together. If the actual work tasks do not offer opportunities, then they need to be created artificially.

Helping others and challenging their opinions is part of the team's work. I do not mean an attitude like "jibing is caring" but pure sparring as in challenging in a positive sense. It is vital that each team understands that an opposite opinion is a means to develop oneself and to ponder one's own ideas more profoundly.

Concrete actions:

☞ *Make a skill chart and place each member onto it*

☞ *Have a meeting where everyone talks about themselves and what they would like to be able to do in the future*

☞ *Agree on what size of a task calls for the opinion of the others*

Each one is to give feedback when asked for it

☞ *Each one completes an Individual-test after which a skill chart is drawn up; a free test is available in Finnish at: www.yhteisoohjautuvuus.fi*

On this stair, it is essential to understand that it is worthwhile to rotate people from task to task, e.g. the compositions of the project team or editorial team. It is easier to switch work tasks when the tasks' technical level of difficulty is low and the team member has room to develop their know-how. An essential and urgent project usually calls for a more skilled member to ensure high quality and efficiency.

REQUIREMENTS

+ Taking the time to teach others

Everyone needs to manage one's time (see the stair Time for Discussion) and understand that part of the work does not necessarily advance one's own tasks. The power of the team

SHARED LEADERSHIP

comes from the fact that we are doing things together, and matters are constantly rotated back and forth between the members.

The team will always have members with different skills and characteristics. This means that one needs to constantly help and guide others. You will also receive help to start with, to develop and to learn. Your own time management must be good enough to be able to give of your time to team members without you yourself feeling stressed or afraid of falling behind.

+ Asking for help even if it isn't actually required

The work easily rewards the worker. When one's own tasks start to flow smoothly, it is easy to forget to ask for help or opinions from others. However, the purpose of the team is to process tasks together. When you get a new task or are pondering solutions, share your know-how with your team. You may be an experienced expert, in which case the solutions to the task's challenges are self-evident for you. Share this information with the others by talking about the challenges and asking for their opinion. Sometimes an expert may get stuck too deep in one's own expertise that the "stupid questions" from a less- knowledgeable team member might inspire simpler and better solutions – or at least prepare for the questions coming from the client.

+ Understanding that the work is done together

For many people working may be an individual performance. However, there are reasons for teamwork, and each team member needs to become aware that work is done together. Everyone has personal working space and time, but the team is brought together for a reason.

If the boundaries set by the team are not compatible with the workflow of a team member, those boundaries should be reconsidered by the team. It is also possible that the person is not suitable for teamwork, and should then be relieved from the team in such a way that they still cooperate with the team without being a member.

+ Changing team compositions and opinions

The team may get into a situation where a task is demanding and the schedule tight. Even if another member would like to learn how to do that task, neither their skills nor their timetable may be enough for it. In these cases, it is important that the experienced member carries out or directs the work, to get it done within the set conditions. On the other hand, there might be a work task that has a more flexible timetable. In this case, it would be more advisable to let the less experienced member perform the task so that they can develop their skills.

Pondering such situations always demands more than one person's point of view. These matters need to be discussed as a pair or among the whole team. The tasks belong to the team, not the individual members. Shifting points of view and discussing matters bring more understanding about the task at hand, the situation, and the general workload of the team.

+ Team members know each other's know-how and skills

There is not always time to discuss everything or to bring urgent matters to the whole team. There may also be situations where some team members are unavailable for several days. Therefore, it is important to know beforehand who knows what. The team should at an early stage map out its members' expertise and what they are interested in developing themselves in. The team should arrange a meeting where each member gets their chance to tell what they know and would like to learn. Based on this, the team draws a skill chart to visualize the know-how of team members at a glance. This chart needs to be updated 4-10 times a year, so that it is always up to date. This skill chart needs to be available for everybody, as it will often be needed urgently when it's necessary to ask for advice or direct a task to another member.

- Everyone works isolated

If the team members do not have time to
help each other, they start to work as individuals inside the team. The
meaning of the team itself disappears. When no help nor opinions are
asked for, experiences cannot be shared and working solo becomes
even more emphasized. A team on the sparring step is to focus on that
the work is really done together, not just seemingly acting as a team
upon the request of the rest of the organisation. If everyone is still
working alone, it must be considered what the problem is, or whether
working as a team just isn't a suitable structure for this type of work.

- Not developing at work

When each member works on their own, they start to do only the tasks
that are the easiest for them. They remain in their comfort zone and do
not take on more challenging work, when thinking that they will not
cope with them. This is only due to not using enough time to communicate with the others nor asking for help or discussing the tasks. At
its worst, halting one's development leads to tasks becoming similar
and losing work motivation. It is very important to have tasks that challenge the person doing them. This leads to a feeling of success after
finishing tasks, which keep you going.

- Not giving the other team members a chance to develop

The lack of communication and not asking for help lead not only to
the above-mentioned threat but also prevents others getting opportunities to develop further at their work. If you are getting familiar and
easy tasks, you could delegate some to your colleagues. There may
be someone in the team who wants to learn those tasks, and the best
trainer is the person familiar with them. The strength of the team lies
in the ability to share work tasks and know-how. If everyone works
isolated, the know-how, neither the success nor the tasks leading to
versatile experience are shared.

- Failing to help a colleague

In case a team member's own time management is not in order and they have not talked about their tasks to the other team members, they end up being in a hurry. A busy team member does not have time to help others nor to participate in team meetings.

It is possible that the team member had not understood the extent of nor the effort required for the task, and because of this they find their timetable is challenging. It is also an indication that the task was not brought to the team for weighing, but the team member just started to carry it out on their own. When someone is in a hurry, it is worthwhile for the team to ease their workload and help each other.

The feeling of not being in control of one's own work tasks makes it difficult to find motivation to help colleagues. If the work is done individually and the know-how is not shared with the others, one may feel "not in the mood" for it. Instead, with teamwork there are always interesting and less interesting tasks. The team itself chooses the tasks, and everyone participates in that choice. If a member does not take an active part in the cooperation of the team, then the tasks do not always feel good.

- Too demanding tasks are chosen

The quality of the work, customer satisfaction, or even the whole team's reputation may suffer from team members being too ambitious and not asking for help from more experienced team members. If the required know-how is not found within the team, it can also be sought from outside the team. While discussing the tasks each member needs to recognize if the task is too challenging. If one thinks that the task is too challenging for a colleague, one needs to be able to talk about that as well in a constructive manner. This is why it is advisable to cross-check the end results of the tasks, so that the others can comment and help each other develop.

Each team member should chart one's own strengths and technical know-how individually. Only after this can the skill chart of the whole team be made. Everyone should make a list, of what direction they want to develop in or what new things might interest them. Based on these lists it is then advisable to make a skill chart e.g., divided into four quarters with two different axiis. Each team member is then placed on the skill chart. After this each member's wishes for development are marked on it. This way a visual reference sheet is created to remind everyone of who knows what and to whom to conveniently pass on a task that is easy for oneself.

The actual chart should be made together at a workshop. Everyone in turn describes their skills and experience – a bit like at a job interview. After this everyone talks about their weaknesses and strengths and about what would interest them in the future. During their presentation the person is placed on the chart based on their skills and wishes for development. At this workshop people get to know each other, their know-how and in what directions members of the team wish to develop. This workshop will also quickly reveal if someone is having motivational problems or has outdated know-how that needs updating.

Only working together never replaces personal coaching, but it does work better than the traditional career development discussion.

There is a lot to communicate about within the team. It is not always possible to bring everything to the whole team, or at least not expect everyone's acceptance or acknowledgement. The team needs to agree on based on the size of tasks when just notifying the rest of the team is enough, when the other team members' agreement is required, and when a separate meeting of the entire team needs to be called. The aim is not to limit freedom, but to make the team understand which matters can be decided upon on one's own.

When a task or an assignment meaningful for the team is considerable enough, it is good to get the opinion of several team members before decisions are made or actions are taken. If it concerns the whole team's tasks for the coming year, it is recommended that the whole team is to be called together to discuss the matter.

This step of sparring may be a burdensome change from traditional teamwork, where most decisions and coordination of tasks are made by a supervisor. To share the leadership, the team constantly faces small conflicts and needs for clarification. After the hardships in the beginning, the team will communicate better, and the rules will feel less confusing or irritating but will start to flow like routine procedures.

Appreciation

When the team members know each other, it will be noticed in the team that pondering the tasks out loud and asking for others' opinions becomes a routine. When the members know each other and work closely together, a "we"-spirit will develop. The identity of the group is born, and in addition to routines mutual habits will also appear.

Team members will start to use phrases like "we", "our team", "in our team" and "let's ask the team". On the fifth step of this team model, the members will be able to endure more feedback from the others and will not be so easily hurt by feedback. Understanding what the colleague is doing, what they know, and what they want to learn creates trust and interest in a new type of cooperation.

Now it is time to weld together the last leaking seams of the team by intentionally creating more mutual habits which commit the team members to each other.

Concrete actions:

- *Show your support to your colleagues and their choices*
- *Do not leave anything undealt with, and bring up even unpleasant matters to be discussed*
- *Celebrate even small successes*
- *Always ask for the opinions of others*
- *Make changes to your actions based on what others say*
- *Bring up any failures at the meetings and learn together from them*

REQUIREMENTS

+ Asking for the opinions of others

Asking for the opinions of others has started to become a routine within the team, even if the person asking already knows what to do. Bringing matters into mutual discussion happens daily. Handling the matters is fast, direct, and professional.

Sometimes matters are brought just for approval, sometimes to get other points of view, and sometimes for to get actual help. The professional know-how is shared by bringing different problems and

solutions to the whole team. If the others in the team suggest other kinds of solutions, it is possible to discuss them straight away and to choose the suitable one for the team.

+ Disputes are not left undealt with

It is not possible to avoid conflicts or disputes between people. Disputes are a normal and expected phenomenon at work and are not to be feared. Disputes just need to be dealt with. The team starts to recognize, according to the situation, when it is better to deal with it right away, and when to deal with it the following day. People who respect each other can yield and find a compromise, even if they disagree on matters. Others in the team will help and support, and they will not turn away or leave.

+ Express that you support the others

Everyone doesn't have to agree on matters, but supporting a colleague is part of teamwork. Bringing up others' good sides and encouraging them increases their motivation and feeling of security. When the team supports its every member they are not as afraid to fail. Thus team members dare to try their best and make personal breakthroughs easier. If everyone is just afraid of failure and the shame of it, nobody ever exceeds oneself.

+ Unpleasant matters are brought up

As a habit of the team all matters which affect the team are brought up. This is not always pleasant, and some matters can be hard to deal with. However, all matters can be dealt with together in a proper manner. For this purpose, the team can do exercises, if for some reason unpleasant matters are kept hidden. For instance, having each member name one point of development for the team or for one's own actions.

+ Celebrating things

Celebrating things is the most important thing. Big and small matters demand at least applause. It is good for the team to learn how to reward itself and each other for a job well done. Even failures can be celebrated, as they always provide a learning experience. By creating a permissive and supportive culture the team's development will be kept constant. When members are not afraid to fail, they feel secure and respected. When members are not afraid to fail, they feel secure and respected. The respect within the team is mostly about patience toward others and sharing matters.

- Asking for advice only when facing problems

If one asks for advice only when there are problems,
the good solutions and know-how do not spread in the team.

The team can never be homogenous, as it is comprised of people. Instead, the quality of the team's actions can be homogeneous when the team communicates and agrees on common principles of action. This can be jeopardized if opinions are not asked and matters are brought forward to the team only when something has already gone wrong or the task has been interrupted.

- Unresolved issues

The activity of the team as a whole is affected If internal conflicts go unresolved. At first e.g. some topics or cooperating with certain people might be avoided. Seemingly small but unresolved issues may lead to a situation where information is not communicated as it should during team meetings. Finally, the team's actions are disrupted, and the conflict hinders the whole team. Motivation decreases and the team members start to feel insecure. This is the last possible moment to resolve the situation. These situations show that it is best to deal with conflicts right away before they cause multiplicative effects.

If not all matters are discussed, the team is not working openly, and as a multiplicative effect the team does not develop anymore. First, issues may seem very small, but in the end the team cannot really even learn from its failures anymore. If the unpleasant themes are avoided for long, the development of the team reverses all the way to the first stair of this model, as the basics are no longer in order.

Shared leadership is created when the team members discuss matters together. Leadership is the result of learning and coming to conclusions together. In a model with a supervisor leadership and decisions rely on only one person, and the quality of the team's actions depends on that supervisor. In a community-led team the whole team is responsible for the goals and quality of its work.

By discussing issues it is possible to learn and make changes to one's own actions. When there is no supervisor to hide things from, each one is responsible for bringing attention to flaws. When another team member is hiding a failure, it is the responsibility of the others to bring it up. Responsibility is carried together in the team, and no freeloaders are allowed. Additionally, it is difficult to be a freeloader when each team member is responsible for leading the work.

Shared leadership forces people to develop as individuals. Everyone needs to learn how to present matters in a constructive way. When matters escalate, there is no supervisor to turn to as a referee. The team must solve the problem internally. Some days may be spent struggling with various matters. Before long the team will solve the problem and also reinforce the team spirit at the same time.

COMMUNITY -LED TEAM

6

Trust

s. 42

7

Shared Viewpoint

s. 45

8

Hive Mind

s. 49

On the last stair of this model the team begins to act independently. The team starts to work as a family with a deep trust despite some everyday friction and a grasp of what everyone wants. Each member of the team may cover for the other, and no internal issues in the team are visible to outsiders.

If the team has a supervisor and decisions need to be run by them, they become a bottleneck for the team's activity and the motivation of the members.

The existence of the team is based on a mutual willingness to reach a goal. This book does not present any demands on this last stair, but shows the characteristics of the team as an outcome of the team's development.

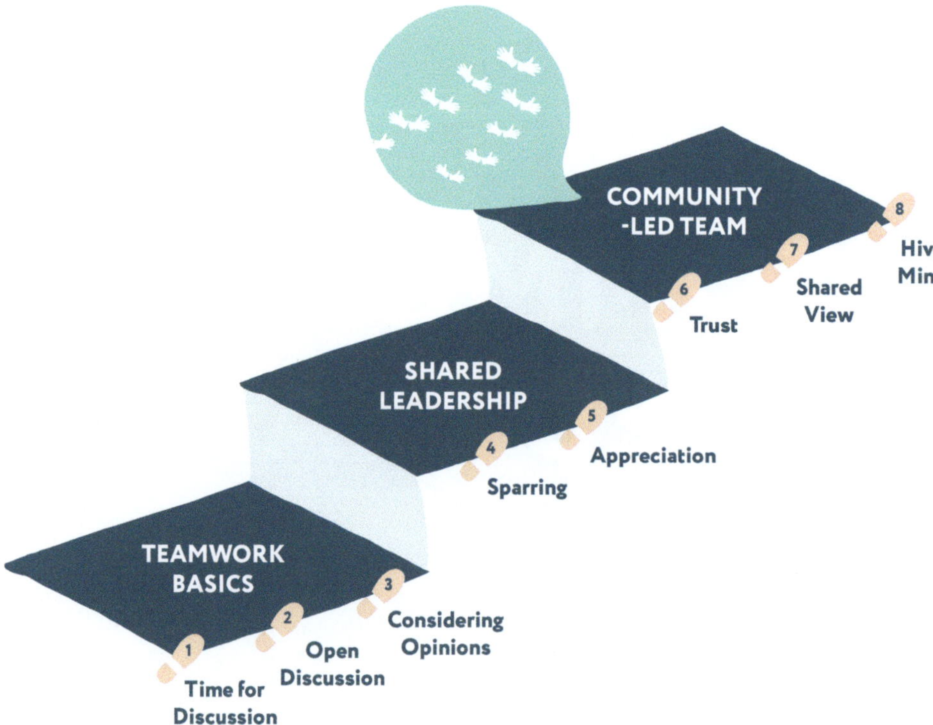

On the highest stair of the model the team works together as a community-led team, has mutual trust, and shares a common point of view.

A community-led team can manage any situation, and the team members have a good feeling about things. The roles and responsibilities inside the team have found their place and the team does not need to focus on building the teamwork, but can instead focus on the actual tasks at hand. The only thing that remains to be done is refining the core of action so that every team member starts to develop as an individual in the context of their work tasks. The development of the individuals happens together with the development of the team, thus improving the performance and know-how of the whole team. When seen from outside the professional competence of the team takes a huge leap forwards when the team reaches the stair of the community-led team.

Trust

The team begins to resemble a family within the frames of the work. There may be some harsh words or friction within the team, but this does not affect the activity and is not visible to outsiders. On this stair, the phenomenon "jibing is caring" might already be applicable. The team itself knows where the limit between togetherness-forming teasing and outright insulting goes. Mutual respect has turned into trust and there is no fear of mistakes or stepping onto others' toes. Giving feedback daily is a norm and openness a habit.

If a team member changes teams or leaves for some other reason, the others will experience feelings of loss. It is normal that emotional bonds have formed between the team members. Each member is committed to the team on the level of actions, work, thoughts, and feelings. Belonging to the team is a common factor of internal motivation, which makes the members proud to belong to this particular team.

Concrete actions:

- ☞ *Challenge others by questioning*
- ☞ *Meet up outside of work*
- ☞ *Learn the names of others' family members*
- ☞ *Learn about others' hobbies*

CHARACTERISTICS

+ Willingness to spend time together outside of work

The team members notice that they are doing things together outside of work-related activities. If the members are childless, young, and active adults, their hobby-related interests might align and the team may spend a lot of time together, even daily. When a member is going through the busy times of being parents to young children, there is not that much free time to spare, but even an activity done once a month outside of work is meaningful.

+ Daring to speak openly about anything

The team has learned to handle even challenging issues together. Trust in the other team members has increased, and the team members have started to share even private matters. It might be about worries, secrets, or something else. Things are shared to make others understand one's situation, or to ask for help in finding solutions. Everyone in the team has learned how effective teamwork is. It is possible to bring up matters that are difficult for oneself to be solved by the team-family. Each team member feels that they are accepted and cared for as the feeling of security inside the team is fulfilled.

+ Constant training

The team has trained to bring matters to to be handled together. The members notice that they are training at everything together. The urge to bring matters to the whole team increases as everything can be discussed. The team members should challenge each other and help them see matters from another angle. The different opinions of others do not seem so difficult anymore nor as personal criticism, but as a chance to develop.

+ Trusting one's colleagues

It would be good for team members to learn the names of their colleagues family members , at least their spouse's name. Each team member should also learn the hobbies of the other members. The greatest trust is built when you know each other and know each other's likes well.

Each team member knows that the other members are there to support them in difficult situations if needed. It does not matter whether it is a work-related or a personal issue at hand. The result is the same if the person loses the ability to work due to a nervous breakdown. On the other hand, it is good to let team members choose how much they want to talk about their private life.

+ Forming work pairs

Everything is not always taken to the whole team, in some cases it is good to have a pair with whom to spar smaller matters into shape. If everyone in a team is working with a different technology or know-how, it is reasonable to form pairs based on mutual interests. The more experienced one is the teacher and the interested one can be an apprentice. Work pairs make the activities more effective and ensure that in case of one member's sick leave the whole team is not paralyzed. There is always someone who knows about the absent person's work tasks, even if are daily team meetings. The work pair can also act as a sub-team.

Shared Viewpoint

The team starts to form its own opinions. Similarly to how everyone knows how their own family would react to something, the team also knows in advance how the team and its members will react.

The team forms its own point of view and identity, which will help the team members to plan and to predict the actions of the team. The target and the goals of the team are all clear to everyone. Everything is based on the team's values, which were created together by each and everyone in the team.

The team understands that it stays flexible when the know-how is as versatile as possible. Everyone starts to figure out the common goal and work towards that. Previously each member has only been able to strive towards one's own personal goals and focus on matters and know-how based on personal interest. On this stair, they begin to understand that one's own know-how needs to be expanded in a direction necessary for the whole team and not just based on one's own interests.

Concrete actions:

☛ *Do things even if not always inspired*

☛ *Bring interesting matters to the team meetings*

☛ *Tell your opinion so that others know what you are thinking*

☛ *Repeat matters and come to conclusions*

CHARACTERISTICS

+ Team members become interested in new things

A spiral of continuous change and development has begun the team. A lot of knowledge has been shared within the team, and everyone's understanding what others can do has increased. The work done together and the results inspire others to get interested in new things. They start to understand what else they could still master.

The emotional bond between the team members reinforces the interest in new things. Common points of interest and action create even more

COMMUNITY-LED TEAM

cooperation between members. Sometimes one may get interested in something only because another team member was interested in it first.

Working in pairs also creates interest in new things. Information about the work pair's interests becomes unavoidable while communicating and working together. When the pair brags about how they have advanced, the enthusiasm easily transfers to the other person as well. After all, the pairs are often formed based on similar interests or tasks, and thus they get easily inspired because of similar interests.

Everyone should bring new matters to the team's common knowledge and meetings. They do not even have to be work-related. It is important that the team members bring up new matters for the team and that these matters are reacted to somehow. When e.g. someone brings a political matter to the meeting, and the reaction is somewhat hostile, it shows what kind of viewpoint the team has on politics. Bringing new matters to the table helps to shape the team's common viewpoint.

+ Keeping up enthusiasm to learn new things

The team members occasionally need to do things that do not feel good. It is often about learning something new or sorting things out. When the big picture, the goal of the team, and the long-term plan are clear in one's mind, the motivation will also endure for performing some unpleasant tasks along the way.

The members' own endurance and energy levels are vital resources for the whole team. When they are nourished, all the members can motivate themselves to even bigger and bigger challenges.

+ Stretching for a colleague

On the lower stairs, it is advised to ask for help, negotiate and spar. On the top stair of the model, the team members are willing to stretch for a colleague in need. The team members may unselfishly offer to do things for others. Often it can be about doing a boring, repetitive task, learning a new thing, or easing the workload of another just to reach the common goal. Helpful deeds are not kept a score of, and nobody gets bitter or annoyed if the favor is not returned or compensated.

+ A common perspective on matters is created

When new matters are brought up for discussion, it is important to draw conclusions out loud. The team members may discuss a matter, and when all seems to have been said, it is time to wrap it up. It means that whoever notices the fading of the discussion begins to reiterate what was said earlier. The biggest differences of opinion are emphasized and finally the team's stance on that matter is stated.

The wrapping-up is probably not carried out by the same person who brought the matter to the team. That person may also be the one member who did not even say that much about it. Practice at wrapping up things unrelated to the team's work can provide experience useful for wrapping up matters of core interest for the team's work.

+ Taking a stand

On the lower stairs of this model, the discussion usually takes place between the team members that are connected to or interested in the matter. When a common viewpoint starts to form, each team member begins to express their own opinion, too. Everybody will comment on the matter, some more, some less, even if the matter is not so interesting to them as such.

Similarly to how everyone at the family dinner table has an opinion, everyone in the team has an opinion when matters are discussed together. It is important that everyone utters their point of view, even if that point of view is not taking a stand about the matter being discussed. The more the members practice communicating, the better their cooperation will work when dealing with challenging matters.

The team has developed a sort of an elevator pitch, which they all know by heart. The team has talked so thoroughly about the basic tasks and activities, so much that everybody has a clear understanding of what the others are thinking. There is a shared view about how the team sees itself and what it is doing. Each member of the team can tell an outsider what the team does, what its strengths are, and what the team members are able to do.

The communication of the team is on such a level that there is no
need for extra effort – the mutual activities have become routines. If
an outsider followed the team's discussion, they would not keep up
with it. The team's communication is comprised of many factors, the
subject may bounce back and forth. Quiet people in fact loud and
suddenly someone not involved in the actual matter at hand may do
a wrap-up of a topic they did not take part in dealing with at all. The
team begins to be ready for the final top step, where the activities of
the team are almost like intuitive reactions to things.

Hive Mind

A community-led team aims to have a hive mind. The team would then act like a flock of birds in flight. When one team member notices an obstacle ahead, they will make evasive maneuvers and immediately communicate about them to the others. Everyone modifies their work, role, and tasks accordingly to avoid the obstacle. From an outside point of view one can see how smoothly the flock of birds avoided the obstacle. Within the flock the tasks, roles and positions were changed literally on the fly.

A community-led team functions the same way in work life and for example in voluntary associations, where rapid reactions are needed.

Fast reactions and decision-making on behalf of others would not be possible without a profound trust between the team members. Everyone should at least superficially know the knowledge and skills of others, so that tasks can be handed to others on the fly. Teamwork is a group sport where individuals don't stand out. The same applies to a community-led team.
The team carries and succeeds.

The internal communication of the team is planned and targeted, even if to an outside observer the evasive maneuvers looked like just reactions to changing conditions. The team has practiced together a lot and has been able to form a shared code of conduct with which it is possible to cope in any given situation.

Concrete actions:

- *Change work tasks with each other*
- *Share daily what is going on for you, share your worries*
- *Practice giving constructive feedback together*
- *Brainstorm together regularly*

+ Work tasks can be switched

Each team member can be covered for
a few days. As the rest of the team is aware of each member's tasks, or
at least the absentee's work pair can talk about the current situation.
By practicing another team member has learned to do at least the easy
tasks in case a given team member suddenly falls ill or otherwise is
obstructed from working normally.

Each team member understands the current situation, so the first
member to notice the absence can communicate about it to the other
team members. The lost time in the traditional model of letting the
supervisor know about absences does not exist as everyone in the
team has the capacity to act and help with the tasks at hand.

+ Recognizing increased workload

Each member of the team can reflect on their own activities and stress
levels. If it starts to be too busy or their work performance is declining,
the team member can ask for help in time. The team meetings and
working in pairs improve the others' understanding of the workload
facing the individual member. If a member does not notice being tired,
the others may help with recognising and easing the burden already
before it turns into an actual problem.

+ Recommending work tasks

The team members know each other's skills and interests, so they can
recommend tasks to each other. Even if previously the nature of the
team's work didn't support switching tasks or "marketing" a colleague,
these things are now becoming possible.

Recommending tasks can exceed the boundaries of one's activities.
People might in work circles recommend leisure activities or freelanc-
er commissions, because everyone knows the interests of the others.
When one knows other's interests and the people as such, one can
understand what the others want from life.

+ Giving feedback

Feedback can be given immediately. There is no place for halting to dwell on guilty feelings, but rather it is a place to learn together. It is not essential who made a mistake, but how to get forward despite the mistake and to improve the team's work.

The team members keep on practicing how to give constructive feedback, e.g. at reflective team meetings. Giving feedback is essential to developing the team and its members. The more the flow of information and feedback rounds become routine, the faster the team learns.

+ React quickly to any change

A community-led team can react quickly to any technological change or changes in the client field. Change is a constant state, which is not a strain but gives gives the opportunity for interesting and versatile activities. The team changes, educates itself, and learns new things on a weekly basis.

When one needs to learn new skills and methods, the team members do not feel that learning is unpleasant nor a burden but just an ordinary part of work, where timetables are agreed on and responsibilities shared by the team.

+ Ideas and achievements are shared

There are no heroes leading the team - cooperation does. When one member comes up with an idea, they bring it to the team for refining and it is made even better together. Individuals do not stand out, but the team works as a unit. Achievements are shared, and they are celebrated together. Nobody is afraid to speak their mind nor to further develop the ideas of other members.

The team is purely community-led when it has several characteristics of the ones above. It is possible that not all of them can be fulfilled due to environmental strains. Because it is about people, there can be a decline and a brief return to lower steps when some requirements are not met. The team may return to a lower step and then develop again. When the hive mind is attained, a temporary drop to lower steps is not a problem. Everybody in the team knows what to do to get work activity back onto the desired step.

Everyday when arriving at work the team members should share how they are doing. It is important for the team members to meet each other and share their state of mind. If people are busy and experiencing a lot of stress from tasks , this stress can be recognized, and some space can be given to others. On the other hand, it does not matter if there were brief pauses in communication, or one member isolated themselves for a while. Usually, after a short time that member returns to the team and explains the reason why they kept their distance for a while.

The team should reflect on its essence and brainstorm its actions on a regular basis. Each team member will grow as a person and improve their technical skills. The team may now serve a certain purpose, but in half a year people's points of interest may change. The team should discuss in what direction it wants to develop and what the goal of the team is.

If the team continues too long with the original plan, the team members may want to leave the team. Sometimes even the team's existence can be questioned. If the team has served its purpose and there is nobody who carries on, it is a perfectly fine option to disassemble the team if everyone agrees to do so.

CONCLUSION

Working with this Model

The team should get together often and regularly, e.g. weekly. Each team member then describes what they did last week, what they are going to do this week, and whether there are any problems or obstacles to those tasks. If there are problems that they cannot solve on their own, the team will help with finding solutions. All matters usually told to a supervisor are now brought to the team. If some matter is delicate, it is possible to handle it in a smaller group first and then decide whether to bring the matter to the whole team.

The shift to a community-led team model with its requirements is not recommended to be brought into the weekly meetings. The daily and weekly meetings are needed for the actual work tasks and focusing on them. The meetings aimed at the development of the team can be organized monthly or four times a year. In these development meetings, the activities of the team are checked, then feedback is given, and requirements and character-istics are pondered upon. These meetings are reflective and thus demand a considerably longer time. Half a day is a good amount of time, and the location should ideally be away from the team's daily premises. Reserve a cabinet room, go to a park, or just get away from the daily work environment. This gives perspective to the themes and a chance to be more relaxed.

Moving Between the Stairs and Steps

At a reflective meeting the team is supposed to recognize on which stair and its step the team is on. The team needs to discuss which step it wants to reach eventually. The team may e.g.decide to reach the stair Shared Leadership within the next half a year. After this a plan to proceed is made, with a calculation of how many weeks the team needs to advance one step.

If the development plan starts to feel too fast, then it is that. Take more time. Getting onto a stair must not be the goal in itself. It is not about the destination, but more about the journey there and what the team members learn along the way. Anyway, the most important task of the team is its core activity, the work itself or those hobby activities that the team exists for.

When a development plan has been made for the team, it is recommended to choose one requirement or property at a time from the model presented in this book. The decisions of the team can then be compared with that requirement or property.

To go through one requirement and rooting that into the team's actions may take a long time. There is no hurry with these, and the team needs to take its time to go through one step at a time.

All members of the team are not likely to be equally interested in the stairs and steps of this model nor the development of the team. It is enough for the development plan that the person responsible for the reflective meeting prepares the meeting. Then some member takes on the task of development voluntarily, or the team decides together who will oversee developing the team. Those who are more interested in working with this model can get deeper into it and then direct the team's development at the reflective meetings. This work should however not be personified with just one person, because then the community-led team model does not work, and the activities start too much to resemble a team with a supervisor leading it.

The Roles

The community-led team takes no stance regarding what kind of roles there are in the team. Usually, the nature and the history of the team's activities dictates what roles are needed. For instance, in a service company there are roles such as customer service, technical performer, and supervisor. In an advertising agency there are roles such as photographer, writer, project manager, and team leader. There are roles if every field, and in a team the roles are divided among team members.

The Rotating Role

Traditionally at team meetings there has been the team leader who guides the meetings through. This role is important and should not be removed. However, this role can be made a rotating role. Routine-like roles are generally good to rotate.

For instance, each weekly meeting is run by a different team leader. Every member of the team gets their turn to facilitate the meeting and lead it. Each meeting resembles its leader, and each team member knows what is required to run a meeting. At the same time everyone learns to respect the others' turns to speak and keeping schedules.

The Conditional Role

If a role contains tasks that nobody wants to perform, it is a good idea to make it a conditional role. Then performing the unpleasant tasks is a prerequisite for being able to transfer the role for the next person. If someone does not perform those tasks on thir turn, they are to keep that role during the next rotation as well.

The Role Based on Volunteering

There may be tasks in the team that only some people are interested in. Those tasks are not shared by all members, but only between those willing, in a way that they themselves see fit. If there is only one willing member, the rest of the team may help that person by defining the time that the task in question will take out of their
working day or week.

The Role Based on Necessity

In an expert organization there are often projects. Projects usually demand a project manager.

For instance, if there are no separate salespeople, each expert acts as a salesperson. In practice, everyone markets their own work and the work of their fellow team members as well. When a customer orders so much work from one person that they cannot handle it alone, then it becomes a team project. When a team member asks for help from the other members, the person asking for help knows the most about the project, so naturally they are the project manager.

The team itself may choose its roles and ways of working. The most important thing is that all matters are agreed on together, and everyone has a chance to Influence these choices. Each person also has the opportunity to say "this matter does not interest me so much, so you are free to decide between you".

Responsibility is often given to the most experienced team member. This is not however an absolute value: sometimes, the top experts may want to focus on a narrow sector of activity.

Communication

The team is to agree together on the communication channels and remember that a choice that turns out to be bad can be quickly changed to a better one. When a team member suggests a new way, it is usually quite effortless to try it out. If that new way of communication, such as chat or WhatsApp, complicates or delays work and does not contribute any added value to it, it can be discarded just as quickly as it was adopted. The most important thing is to find functional ways to share information and follow team members and their tasks.

It is advised for the team to have a a group or tool for instant messaging, something like WhatsApp, Telegram or Kaizala. However, everyone needs to remember that the instant messaging group is like a corridor chat. Those speaking are also those listening. A discussion getting hundreds of comments in mere hours cannot be the only nor the most important channel for communication and information. The whole team also does not have to be in the same group, but separate instant messaging groups can be formed inside the team according to different topics.

For proper communication it is worthwhile to use discussion-based tools like Teams and Slack. There it is possible to create channels, rooms, or spaces according to different clients or activities. Current information is gathered there and those involved are marked. This way the silent know-how is uncovered from closed discussions to be found easier. Even if the discussion was only between two members, a third person interested in it can join if they wish. This is not possible in a chat group if the team member is not in the group in question. Another good side is that later, when returning to the matter, that discussion is available for everyone and not just in closed discussion groups.

Information technology and text-based channels are practical and make life easier, but there is also a trap. Some complicated matters are better to discuss and decide at a face-to-face meeting rather than rolling it back and forth for days in some instant messaging channel. When the matter is not progressing or the members involved do not have the energy to focus on reading about the details in the chat thread, everyone has a duty to organize a meeting and decide the matter.

E-mail is used mainly when some of the above-mentioned tools are not in use. That can be the case with a new client or just communicating outside the team. As a tool e-mail is often the least effective and its information security the worst. It is not recommended as the main internal tool for communication for the work community.

If there is only one recipient and the message starts to extend into several sentences, it might be better to call instead. A personal meeting facilitates working and positive interaction considerably. During a busy workday it is usually pleasant to hear a colleague's voice, whether on a small or big matter. Prefer the human approach and always take the recipient into account.

Document management is part of communication. Choose a secure, proper tool, and do not send files via instant messaging or e-mail. Put the files on cloud platforms, where access rights are set up just for the team members. After that you can send links, so that team members always get the latest version of the file. This way the file can be found via search functions in its proper place. If the message gets to the wrong recipient, they will not be able to see the document as it has been protected by access rights restrictions.

Measuring Activities

It is worthwhile to measure the team's activities and its overall feeling constantly. The measuring needs to be quick and easy to perform. A good option is e.g. an electronic multiple-choice survey that each team member fills out, e.g. on Mondays. The goal is to make it so short that filling it in barely takes a minute. As an example, answer the following questions on a scale of 1 to 5:

- **How are you feeling?** *(1 = bad, 5 = really good)*

- **Your level of workload** *(1 = no work, 5 = too much work)*

- **Open comment**

The measuring survey should ideally be automated so that the time invest-ment to send it and to fill it out is minimal. The team can agree that the per-son in charge of arranging the meeting will always check the answers before the meeting and read the written feedback.

The results of the measuring survey are viewed at the team meeting. If the feeling or the workload is 3 or below, it needs to be discussed. By default the mean values should be 4 or above. If the results are lower, things must be discussed, and it should be considered what could be done. It is important that the team has a good feeling, and even smaller slumps in the workload or feeling need to be noticed. They must be reacted to quickly, even in the same week, and remedial actions should be taken.

A constant heavy workload or hurry causes stress at work. The work situa-tion must not be continuously burdensome. Naturally, sometimes there may be situations where the team needs to work harder for a week or two. After that a normal or even a lighter week is needed to recover. If the workload keeps on being too heavy, the team needs to think whether there is a lack of workers in the team. Then, the team needs to recruit more workers or reduce the amount of work so that everyone has a suitable workload.

The team may also develop other measurements for its activities. The team itself knows what the team members need and what needs to be measured. Once a month there can be a larger measuring survey, but principally the sur-veys need to be quick to fill in. The type of measuring must also be accepted by all the team members. It must not disturb nor is burden any of the team's work, and it must have another purpose besides just measuring for its own sake. When the team itself has decided upon the measuring and understands its purpose, everyone finds the motivation to fill in the survey form.

Modern technology can provide other means of measuring rather than the traditional link in an e-mail. Sometimes measurements or the team's overall feeling can be fun to measure with a pin board or with Post It -stickers if the team has daily meetings physically in the same space. The team can get creative with measuring and use whatever tools, as long as most of the team members are committed to it.

CLOSING WORDS

The model for a community-led team is not a new invention, yet it follows the trends of today. Teamwork itself is familiar to people. On free time, like on trips to the summer cottage, many of us can act like in a community-led team, despite never having heard about this model.

Usually, work life sets more limitations for cooperation, actions, and timetables than free time does. To work effectively together, we need to set some common ground rules.

Humanity and consideration for others must be the highest priorities when working together. When one keeps that in mind, one cannot step astray from the community-led path. This book presents the model in a simplified way to show how a team acts and communicates. This model is a tool for recognising how to improve activities. The model is not aimed at causing any stress or pressure to anyone to perform more in the team, but just to remind how to work together and agree on common rules.

The model can be enriched, if desired, by adding an advisory process. In an advisory process each member in the organization has a right to make decisions, as long as they involve those members who are directly affected by that decision. In that case nobody can later claim "you decided" as everyone was given a chance to influence the matter. If it wants, the team may agree to take on an advisory process if another way of making decisions is found burdensome or some clarification is needed.

Other possible ways to make decisions are a process of notification, sharing responsibilities, democracy, consent, and consensus. If it wants, the team may look for information about other ways of decision-making and then apply them.

According to my own experience, the decision-making in teams is natural and easy-going. Sometimes one needs to repeat the rules but usually a precise analysis of the decision-making only makes matters worse. However, it is in the nature of a team to try out what the team members suggest.

The team needs to be open and adaptable. When it is time to experiment, feel free to try things out without prejudice. The biggest obstacles for development are individuals, not tasks or processes. Remember well-being and a reasonable pace in your activities, and the rest will easily follow.

Author website:
www.johtajuushakkeri.fi/en